Brading Community Archive Group (BCAG) was fo
volunteers after the death of Brading local historian Molly Pewsey. Molly came to
the Island in 1970 and taught history at Sandown High School and Medina High
School, as well as working in her spare time as Brading's unofficial local historian.
She collected photographs, documents and in 1995 she began to record oral
histories and memories of older Brading residents. The snippets in this book have
been taken from these and other oral accounts.

Just before her death in 2014, Molly bequeathed her collection of heritage
documents to Cathy Mills, who had just retired after many years as Brading's Town
Clerk. Cathy had many conversations with Dr Ruth Waller, who was then working
on a Brading Heritage Audit for the Town Council's work on the Brading
Neighbourhood Plan. These conversations centred on what should be done with
Molly's archive and how to continue work on Brading's history and provide
opportunities for young people to learn about their heritage. The result was the
creation of BCAG in partnership with the Brading Town Trust and Brading Town
Council with the aim of putting together a Heritage Lottery Fund (HLF) bid called
'Unlocking the Vaults'.

The BCAG has also been successful in bidding for funds from the East Wight
Landscape Partnership's 'Down to the Coast' for a separate project sharing Molly
Pewsey's heritage legacy and other sources. Using the contents of Molly's
collection together with other artefacts and pictures held by individuals and by
Brading Town Trust, the BCAG has endeavoured to compile a book which illustrates
how life for Brading citizens has changed during the last 150 years.

The intention in this book is not to write a history of Brading, but rather through
individual perceptions and images to give an impression of what it was like to live in
Brading towards the end of the 19th century and into the 20th century. Much of the
text in this book directly reflects the memories of former residents of Brading.
Often these people were reflecting back over many years and their memories may
have become distorted, which raises the possibility of historical inaccuracies.
However, we believe that the value of these personal recollections far outweighs
the disadvantages in presenting a record of life in Brading.

The initials before each quote identify the speaker and a key to contributors is on
page 104.

The photos and memories are arranged as a walk around Brading, beginning with the entrance from Ryde, past the Church with a detour to Quay Lane, back along the High Street and around the Bull Ring and West Street. Resuming in the Bull Ring and along New Road to Yarbridge, along by Hornsey Rise into the Mall and back to the Bull Ring.

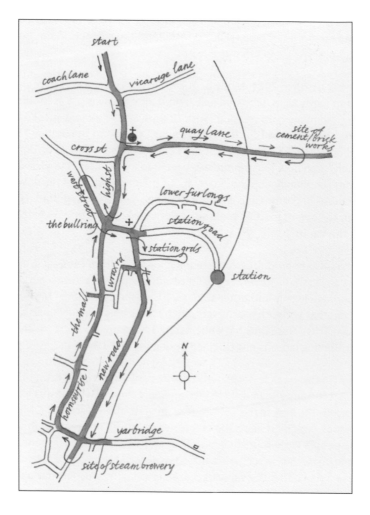

Our starting point is the journal of Miss Sarah Emma White, (the daughter of a Brading master grocer) who was born in 1844 and clearly described life in Brading during the second half of the nineteenth century.

Approaching Brading from Ryde

(SEW) "I consider it an important town. In my younger days, it was governed by Mayor and Corporation. The harbour was a busy place the coal boats coming up to the quay. My father coming in about breakfast time with a long string of flatfish he had caught and boys coming round with cockles they got there and doing a good trade with them. I remember poor old Neddie Osman who lived in the hulk of a smuggler's old vessel. Coming up the lane from the harbour, then called Wall Lane, was the Pound where stray animals were locked up. This joined the churchyard opposite the vicarage then occupied by the Rev Dunbar Isidore Heath (vicar from 1847-1862), who kindly gave me French lessons at 6 am. He was afterwards tried at the Court of Arches and had to leave the church. He preached on the outside doorstep of the Church and on Brading Downs on Sundays where he had a very large congregation."

(JL) "I was born in March 1921 and lived at Rowborough Farm. My dad's sister, Mrs Squibb, lived in the next cottage, they had seven children who used to walk me to school when I was 5. In those days there were trees all the way into Brading right from the railway bridge, it was full of birds and the road used to be covered with white spots. A real rookery there. In the first week of May there was a rook shoot. Lots of people used to eat them, but we never did. Mrs Morgan and Mr Young, they used to be down at The Russells in Brading, they loved them."

Approaching Brading, from an early glass negative

(HW) "I remember the horse and carts and all that. We used to play football out in the road. We used to station someone out top of Church Hill. They'd shout 'Car coming' and then you'd have about a quarter of an hour before the next one came."

A very early photograph (c.1870) of Brading Church before restoration

Brading National School (C of E). Built 1823. William Long left £300 to build a school for use "in the principal of the Established Church". 'Infants' added later. School House built 1846.

(JR) "I was at the Church School. Where the car park is now, there was thirteen gardens because it was church land then. If you were ten years old and interested in a garden, you were given a garden and you had two afternoons to go and work the garden under 'Gubby' Hawkins. You had to keep your garden up together or it was taken away from you. You had to put a collection of vegetables in the Agricultural Show up there or you'd lose your garden, and that is where I got my grounding for gardens. I won my first rake and hoe up there."

(HW) "I went to school where the youth club is, that was the village school. Started off with teacher Bessie (taught 1894-1944), she done the young ones, then Miss Marrow then 'Gubby' Hawkins as we used to call her, she lived in The Limes."

(JS) "Lovely teacher, Teacher Bessie. Miss Griffin lived in the High Street with her mother and sister. Our school days were very strict and we had to behave ourselves. One day we had to take a packed lunch, we hung it up in the porch under our coats and our little bags while we were in the school. The Vicarage was in Quay

Lane and they kept pigs and all sorts, and the pigs got out and ate our lunches (c.1908). Vicar at that time was Mr Blenkin (1906-13) and he had to go and get us more sandwiches."

Calvert 1846 aquatint

Original Town Hall and Jail 1730 until restoration in 1876.
Before the building of the first school in 1823, the children were taught in the Town Hall, and it was also used for Mother's Meetings.

(SEW) "I have seen some very grand funerals both inside the church and in the churchyard with lovely ostrich feathers on the horses and grand plumes on the hearse and mourning coaches. The mutes with their staves draped in black standing on each side of the procession to pass through, and the men with long flowing silk hat bands. The fine old church in my young days had tall square pews and was lighted with tallow candles. On the dark evenings people carried lanterns to Church and left them in the porch, the women wore pattens and clogs in dirty weather which also were left in the porch. We had no hymn books but always sang the metrical psalms at the end of the prayer book."

The Old Town Hall was restored to its present state in 1876. Brading was formerly the testing place for weights & measures for all of East Wight and these standards are still kept in the upper building together with the Town Charter.

Early photograph of men with the Hospital Sunday Banner and collection boxes

Hospital Sunday collection box in the Old Town Hall

(SEW) "To the front of the churchyard was the Town Hall upstairs in the Market House, and the old lock up where the prisoners would peep out at the top between the bars. The Stocks and Whipping Post are still to be seen."

From Kelly's Directory in 1904: The Old Town Hall was rebuilt on its old site in 1875-6 and is a picturesque structure of stone and brick, resting on the south side on open arches, and within this portion, underneath the hall are kept the ancient stocks and whipping post; at the north there is a lock up: in the hall there is a free library containing 1700 volumes, and supported in part by private subscriptions: on the west side of the building is a stone panel bearing a representation of the old borough seal – a Tudor rose, with a legend, 'The Kyng's Towne of Brading'. Opposite the Town Hall are two timber framed houses, and over the door of one of these appears the inscription, 'William Sothcot 1698'.

The changing view south from an old photograph and one taken in 2017

2017

(FTJ) "Crossing the road is the junction of Wall Lane (more generally remembered as Quay Lane) and the High Street. At that junction are still some really very old houses. When I first knew them they were the property of a wonderful old lady by the name of Carley. I think there are still some descendants of her living."

Entering Quay Lane

The War Memorial in St Mary's churchyard was dedicated on Sunday 3rd April 1921 by the Bishop of Southampton. It was designed by Mr Percy Stone and the figure of Christ was sculpted by Mr Nicolls of Kensington. The memorial records the names of 34 Brading men killed in the Great War (WW1) and one from Yaverland, named Frederick Butchers, killed at Mons in 1914 who was considered "practically a Brading Boy" (from Vestry Minutes).

2017

The base of the sundial is medieval with a shaft dated 1714 whilst the sundial on top is dated 1815. The stone post is thought to be the remains of the old churchyard cross.

Postcards of St Mary's Churchyard and the grave of 'Little Jane' c.1900

In the mid 1940s, when Brian was about 14, he and his brother climbed the church spire when they were re-pointing it. They had permission from the vicar to climb the scaffolding. Safety instructions were "to hold on tight and keep climbing!"

(JH) "You know I've seen that man, 'Doughie' Buckett, go right up on that cock on top of the church, he could go up and come down. He used to dig all the graves up there. He could go up the side of that church just strapping ladders on as he went up there. No fear at all."

Brian Berry

View from the top of the church from a postcard and a photograph of Brading from the Downs c.1840

The Bell Ringers of St Mary's Church Easter 1906
P Dowden, Price, Wally Cooper, Simmonds, Attrill, Shaver Pain,
Wavell Pain, JM Taylor, Fred Bench, Mark Squibb,
Fred Jolliffe, George Wilkins

Members of
the Brading
Mothers'
Meeting at the
Vicarage in
Quay Lane
c.1900
(Rev Summers
far left)

2017

2017

The Auction House was one new business which was created with the redevelopment of the Waxworks site.

2017

Brading Gun Shed in the churchyard was restored in 1983. The brass gun was given to the town by King Edward IV in 1549. The last time it was fired was in 1842 on Brading Down when the barrel split. The gun is currently at Nunwell.

(BH) "My grandfather had a market garden where it slopes down right to the railway near Stitchbury, that's been a market garden for a long time down there. He used to have pigs and chickens. He used to have the first early potatoes, underneath that cliff wall - they were absolutely marvellous. He used to grow everything and he had a horse and cart, used to go round to Seaview, Bembridge, St Helens and Gran used to make potted meats and brawn. Used to make beautiful potted meats, tasted heavenly. She was a very clever person. It was a wonderful garden he had there. Another thing Granddad used to grow was violets, I have never seen stems like it, used to be that long and huge, had rows and rows of them and people would go for a bunch of violets for about threepence. This is just before the war (1930s).

2017

The Pound in Quay Lane was built about 200 years ago to enclose straying animals. A fine had to be paid to reclaim them.

(JR) "The old cement, brick works and lime place at the bottom of Quay Lane - as a school boy we played in the pit at the weekends. There was a huge pit really deep and the men working down there had a cable pulley up with about six small buggies on. They used to dig it out and load up the trolleys and take them up by donkey engine and pulled up to where they were tipped into the crusher and from there they went into various departments for making into bricks and cement. At weekends, when there was hardly any one about, we used to go down and get up in the buggies and have a rundown. It was a funny old place, it always reminded us of a ruin but there must have been at least 15 men working down there. The beauty of it was they had a whistle or a horn on the cement works, it used to go off 7:30 in the morning to warn them for 8 o'clock to start, 12 o'clock dinner time, 1 o'clock back to work, and then again at 5 o'clock so nobody in Brading needed a clock 'cos you had hooters down there. At that time they used to use mostly coke for the firing of the kilns and that was all brought in by the railway and just there, there are three sets of rails one from Brading, St Helens and Bembridge which was the local train. The other one was for shunting spare carriages and trucks where a lot were kept, and one was for the cement works. They used to come in alongside the big wall down there and they had three

Aerial view c.1928

openings which was great big steel flaps that used to come down and they used to come across the footpath on that side of the openings, then all the coke was wheeled from there by barrows into their coke holes. They used to have half a dozen trucks at a time that used to come in, apparently they used to come in from St Helens Quay across from Hayling Island. I don't remember seeing coal I think most of it was coke without a doubt."

Demolition of the cement works, chimney and setting the charge c.1950

View north from an early 20th century postcard

View west from the Churchyard from a 19th century glass negative

Returning to the High Street

Early 20th century postcard showing the view west from Quay Lane

Joe Nash (1843-1930) outside his home. The bowl beside him in summer held information for passers by. He also sold potatoes.

(CW) "German Richards lived here in the 16th century and brewed beer for the sailors at St Helens." (FTJ) "The property consisted of dwelling accommodation, a shop and a large barn-like building which as far as I know was practically unused for many years. That has now been converted to a dwelling."

September 1965

Old Town Hall and Rectory Mansion today

2017

Early and mid 20th century photographs at the top of the High Street

(KW) " 'Baccy' Reid's shop there, opposite the stocks, used to sell fireworks but he wouldn't let us have them 'cause we were underage, used to sell shoes as well, and he'd put the fireworks in a shoe box until the day. We went with my brother to get them."

Waxworks postcard c.1970

(JL & BH) " 'Baccy' Reid had a little shop near the church with a sign up 'Get Your Back Scratcher Here'."

(BH) "Mr Carley had a shop where the Waxworks is and Mrs Carley used to make custard ice cream she used to stand it outside in a little urn, and it was absolutely lovely."

The Waxworks first opened in 1965, under the ownership of Graham Osborn-Smith. It had a large collection of taxidermy exhibits and historical artefacts as well as numerous waxwork tableaux. It was renamed 'Brading: The Experience' by new owners in 2005. It was closed in January 2010. Rectory Mansion is now (2017) an 'Antique, Vintage & Retro Emporium'.

(SEW) "There was no pavement only a narrow kerbed footpath, and so muddy after rain. Four horse coaches came to and from Ryde to Ventnor at stated times they sounded a horn to tell of its approach. The postman doing the same in his red coat at 7 pm. There were fairly good shops in Brading. Mrs Wavell lived at the town end of Wall Lane and kept a dairy. Mr Wavell had coal sheds, next to them was Mr Carley with Island views and ornaments peculiar to the Island, Legh Richmond's little Book, etc. Mr Blake opposite the church had a dairy, lower down the street Humphrey's small shop, baker and grocer, farther down on opposite side, Miss Langley, baker and grocer's shop, and a few more houses and my father's grocer and shoemaking establishment, then Mr Humphrey with dairy and coal stores. Dr Atkinson's where ordinary medicines could be had, Mr Wheeler's draper and grocer. Mrs Wheeler also marine stores, crockery, simple medicines and ironmongery. Mr Samuel Midlane ironmonger. Mr Wm Humphrey tailor, Mrs Wilburn, a small sweet shop through the wicket gate on the road to The Mall. Old Mr Riddick, a Scottish gentleman, baker and grocer near the Bull Ring. Mr Stone draper on The Mall, Mr Herbert boot and shoemaker, Mr Bench baker and grocer's shop, had a different appearance then, the candle rack secured to the ceiling, tallow candles hanging in pounds of 8, 10, 12 and 14, also rush lights. Loaf sugar sent in loaves, nothing in packages. The weekly newspaper cost fourpence, several neighbours paid one penny to take their turn to read it. Envelopes had no gum, they were fastened with wafers of sealing wax. Brading Fair was held on May 2nd and 3rd, and October 13th and 14th. There were long tables in several places on the kerbed footpath laden with nuts, oranges, apples, stewed pears in saucers, gold trimmed pieces of gingerbread in various designs, games, the dice box for which a halfpenny a throw was charged. The children made a practice of going

shroving on Shrove Tuesday. On November 5th there was a procession through the town with Guy Fawkes seated in an old armchair and finally committed to the flames in a huge bonfire on Brading Down."

(FTJ) "Almost at the top of the hill, there were horse stables and the appurtenances for coal merchant and dairy farmer. The coal merchant and dairy farmer have gone and the stables have been changed into dwelling houses, the other new residences have been built."

Deacon's butchers and vegetable shop, now an estate agents

(GP) "I remember Deacon's shop they sold rabbits, pigeons, anything."
(MP) "GP mentions the items hanging up outside the shop front with Mr Deacon standing nearby."

2017

Hospital Sunday

(BPM) 1893 included this reference: "September 3rd was our Harvest Festival. A suggestion was made to the vicar that there should be a Church Parade of the Friendly Societies of the district for morning service and the matter was warmly taken up. At 9.30 am, the Brading members met on the Station Road and went to Morton to meet the southern contingent, who were accompanied by the Sandown Town Band. A house to house collection was made on the route as well as on the return for the Isle of Wight Infirmary."

(BPM) September 1895, details how it had gained momentum: "On Sunday there was, as last year, a Church Parade of the Friendly Societies of the district, the Foresters attending from Ryde, the Odd Fellows from Sandown, and the Hampshire Friendly Society from Brading beside others. The ancient town was perambulated to the enlivening strains of the Sandown Town Band and a house to house collection made. The bells rang out a joyful invitation and the service, in which the band kindly took part, was bright and hearty. £20 has been forwarded to the Infirmary."

Thus started an important annual event for Brading, which became known as "Hospital Sunday" and continued for decades raising funds for the Isle of Wight County Hospital at Ryde, which was then dependant on voluntary contributions.

The band of the Isle of Wight Rifles (c. 1916) march to St Mary's Church on Hospital Sunday. The Scouts can be seen marching behind the banner. Two local men Mr Cox and Mr Gladdis (with beard) head the procession, each wearing their official collector's rosette. The local policeman walks beside them. The author of "The Isle of Wight Rifles", Mr D.J. Quigley, states that the bandsmen are wearing the khaki uniform that they adopted at the start of World War I and that the second battalion went from Parkhurst to Nunwell Park in 1916 and completed their training with the Duke of Cornwall's Light Infantry.

In later years, Mr Jim Scott (JSc) recalls that "the procession started from the Bull Ring went via New Road to Yarbridge and that the big base drummer had to stop playing as they climbed the hill to the Congregational Church! Once down the Mall, they proceeded through the High Street to the church. Jim recognises Mr Harbour (front left wearing a straw hat and carrying a cane) The procession was headed by the Brading Town Band followed by the Hospital Sunday Banner, a huge square banner almost as wide as the High Street manned by two stalwarts carrying the poles, one at each side with two men at the front and two at the rear steadying the banner with a stout tasselled cord each. Collections were taken by dozens of helpers along the route and every household was called upon. Collections went on around the Old Town Hall until dusk and the collecting boxes had to be taken many times to the upstairs Council Chamber to be emptied."

Hospital Sunday Celebrations

(KW & CB) "Of course the Vicarage Fields was always used for sport and everything. I remember going down there in the Silver Jubilee (1935), everyone had their mugs given. The nurses were there in Hospital Week, they stayed up at the top of the road there. Johnny Harwood from Cross Street had a gramophone on a pram, that was the music then 'cause they had Brading Town Band before then."

The Hospital Sunday Banner on display at the BCAG Exhibition in the New Town Hall November 18th 2017

(GP) "On the pavement outside the baker's shop (now the Doll's Museum) was the water pump which provided natural water all year round. You had to pump half a bucket of water first, tip it out, and then pump again."

(KW & CB) "We used to have the wheels off the old prams and make these go carts. I've seen as many as nine come down Church Hill and try and turn in on the right hand side by the stables, little shop there now. They'd try and get round, perhaps six would get round and it would gradually get tighter and tighter, and the last ones would hit the wall. Used to take your front wheel out, you'd stick your back with your bolt onto the one in front, so every one had two wheels except the leader who had four. There was nothing about hardly then, perhaps only see three cars all day long."

Comparative views from a postcard c.1900 and 2017

1905

Herbie Wetherick lived with his mother at 32 High Street and when he was about five years old his mother bought the Bakehouse which is now the Doll's Museum. "We had a water pump out of the back here for the three houses, there was one outside the Bakehouse and one up by Sydney Cottages there."

2017

The Lilliput Doll and Toy Museum 2017

(HW) "The Bakehouse was a grocery as well and that side window in the wall used to be the sweet shop, used to sell sweets to the kids as they went to school. When I left school I went to the Bakehouse there, learned to do the dough and that. When I was about 17 or 18 years old we had 'dos' in the Bakehouse after it was all shut up. We used to have musical evenings and we would all get round and people would come and buy crisps and we'd get the music going like a club. It had half doors. I used to get spare bits of dough and make them like a roll and hand it out to kids coming from school. They'd hang over the door and I'd say 'Here take that home'."

(SEW) "A short distance down the hill from the church in the lane to the right stood the Bryanite chapel, a long narrow low building always crowded and so badly ventilated that it was sometimes difficult to keep the candles burning, the services were very lively usually."

This shop window is now part of the Bugle Inn

BH remembers that George Simmonds sold cooked meats and had big green vases of gladioli and carnations on the stone-flagged floor. The three cottages on the right of the shop were pulled down after the 1939-45 war. They had belonged to Mew Langton Brewery. Mr Harbour lived there as did Jack Rock. The rent had been 10 shillings (50p) a week. Arnold's Yard was at the back of the houses.

(AKM) "Before the sub post office in Brading was opened in 1850, the Bugle Inn was used for collecting and delivering letters. Incoming letters used to be placed in the window for people to come and take them. A letter box was placed in the window for outgoing mail and two or three times a week the mail coach would come on its way to or from Ventnor. In 1840 'Letter Carriers' were employed to carry the mail to various parts of the Island. Brading residents, so it was said, were fond of gossip in those days and people, jealous of their correspondence, made so many complaints that a sub post office was established in 1850 in a 15th century cottage on the east side of the High Street near the Bull Ring."

2017

(FTJ) "There were, on the right hand as one approaches the hill leading up to the church, several cottages, the first two of which were built below pavement level and one had to descend a step or two to enter the house. How the occupants fared when there was a heavy downpour of rain, I have often wondered. Two houses stand there now Willow Cottages were the names given them when built, but now renamed St Joseph's and Dolphin Cottage. Other cottages were standing next to them. The land is now used as a car park. At the side of the park is a right of way to what is known as the Withy Bed."

2017

(HW) "Miss Marrow lived over the road where the car park of the Bugle is, used to be houses. Used to be an arch over what we call 'Arnold's Yard'. There was a gap between the houses where we used to go down to the Marsh, what we called 'Barley Cut'."

(BH) "The Bugle was a Mews Langton (brewery in Newport). The stables were where the shop is opposite The Bugle. The coaches and things used to go in there, that's all to do with The Bugle."

(MP) "This building (The Puppet Cabin, The Secret Garden) was once known as The Barn because of the barn at the rear. It was built of stone in 1699. It has had a variety of uses during its long history."

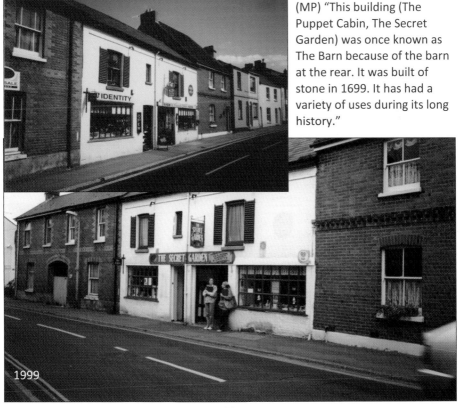

1999

Mr Percy (Pasha) Buckett outside the Gas Showroom 1930

(KW) "He came round with his long pole to switch the gaslights on and off."

2017

The Gas Showroom became a branch of the National Bank (later NatWest) before becoming a private dwelling in the 1980s

The building now known as Kynges Well has housed a number of restaurants and a pottery. At different times it has been known by many names including Goulds, Woodlands, the Red Lion (twice), the Black Horse, the Snooty Fox, A la Carte and Badgers Bistro.

(MP) "It was once a Temperance House! There is a well inside the building with an old pump, which used to be outside the building, dated 1764."

Ye Olde Red Lion.

Licensed Restaurant.

2017

31

Late 19th century photograph looking north. Rochdale House is the shop with the baskets outside.

(HW) "Where Nancy Stay's shop used to be, they used to hire out cycles and all that for 3d or 4d a time, for an hour. I used to have a go on that. They used to have a petrol thing out there and all just outside on the pavement, used to sell petrol."

(HW) "Brading was busier then in the twenties and thirties than what it is now. There were bigger families for a start and shops all down the High Street. Shops opposite our bakery, Chaffey's. Further down there was Simmond's and then there was Eddie Huck, then Stay's, furniture shop (Miss Hewson's), Riddick's then Redstones' on the opposite side. 'Putty' Newman down this side, bootmaker up there as well, Taylor's, 'Doughie' Buckett, sweep, lived in the High Street on the right going down, opposite Bugle car park, kept his soot in West Street. He used to be a baker in the navy that's why we called him 'Doughie'."

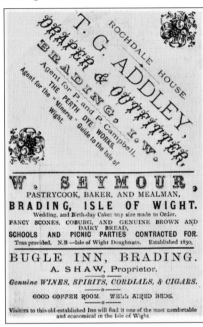

Rochdale House as Tony Nixon's Antique Shop before he converted it into a private dwelling

2017

Mr Gladdis outside his shop
c.1920

Together with the adjoining house, it was formerly known as Rochdale House. When they split, the other house kept the name.

Miss Florence Hewson

In the 1930s, Mrs Hewson ran a sweet shop and guest house for cyclists during World War II. She took in members of the RAF working at St Boniface Down Radar Station. Her daughter 'Flo' later took over the sweet shop until the 1990s.

2017

William Russell of Yaverland built The Russells in 1623 as his town house. Later, in the 19th century, it became a community and reading room.

(HW) "In the thirties and forties we used to have quite a few people stay in Brading in the summer at The Russells, we used to rent out one bedroom for The Russells, if they didn't have enough room, used to sleep'em out see, always used to be filled up."

(JR) "Most of the houses in Brading had a well in their back gardens. Gran had a well in the back of her garden, a hell of a well it was. I remember seeing it cleaned out and it was brick, all brick lined like a bottle, beautiful made, and you wanted a hell of a ladder to get down. On Sundays, I can always remember going to the well in the High Street and getting a jug of water, there used to be a little lace thing with beads over the top to keep the flies away."

Ivy Sears and Dora Grapes just before the pump was removed.

36

The Village Pump Brading. I.W. 478.

(SEW) "The doors of many of the cottages were fitted to open with leather straps and pulled in when no company was wanted."

The same view today

2017

(CB) "Brading Post Office was a sorting office. The outgoing mail was sorted, postmarked and the postman used to take the bags of mail to Brading station for carriage to their destination. Henry Loe was the postmaster and the postmen were 'Socker' Bench and John Stribling. It was a well known sight for 'Socker' to be delivering the High Street mail and see him reading the postcards as he went along,

'pince-nez' glasses on the end of his nose."

Robert Loe was also listed as a clockmaker. This example of his work is in Newport Records Office.

From Kelly's Directory in 1904: Henry Loe, postmaster High Street. Letters and parcels are delivered at 7 & 11.10am & 6.15pm; dispatched at 10.25am & 1.15 & 8.30pm; parcel post dispatched at 8pm.

(BH) "Henry Loe was a watch repairer as well and if he was in the middle of repairing a watch you'd have to wait until he was finished."

(AKM) "A sub post office was established in 1850 in a 15th century cottage on the east side of the High Street, near the Bull Ring, Mr Robert Loe, who owned the property, joined the Post Office in 1850 and carried on over 60 years - part of the time as Post Master at Brading.

His son, Henry Loe, began work in the Office at age 15 and, after his father's death, was Post Master at Brading for 38 years, retiring at the age of 82 in 1939; he died in that same year, just before the outbreak of the second world war. Mrs Julia Mary Loe, Henry's wife, carried on working as post mistress for a short period during Henry's illness until the Post Office was transferred to the Bull Ring site and was run by a Mr Harvey. Mr Henry Loe was visited by an IOW Times reporter in 1939. He described Mr Loe as a tall, grey- moustached man, with a bold firm chin. The Vectis Directory for 1839 notes that the horse drawn coaches used on the IOW were 'Rocket', 'Royal Mail', 'Royal Telegraph' and the 'Quicksilver'."

One of four buses imported from Worthing for the 1905 season (April to October). They were adapted to allow the carrying of parcels and mail.

Miss Black outside the shop

(GP) "Miss Black's mother had a sweet shop when I was a kid just down below the butcher's shop. Used to be the butcher's, then Mrs Rainer lived just where those steps are, Brading Post Office next door, Mr Loe, Mrs Black had a sweet shop there. There was another little cottage, Taylor's the boot repairer there. Mrs Black came to run the sweetshop in about 1931. There used to be Jonathon Riddick's where the Spar shop is. There used to be a bank down there next to Miss Hewson's - Little Lloyds I think it was called."

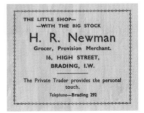
39

HRH Edward Prince of Wales passing through Brading c.1926

Brading Sack Race. Boxing Day 1948. Gordon Trott (white spot) in the lead and
eventual winner

O H Brading butcher's shop and to the left the Post Office, W Stay tobacconist and ironmonger and (with the awning) Riddick and Sons c.1930

GO TO
O. H. BRADING,
PURVEYOR

For Home Killed and Imported Meat.
Best Quality and Service.

BULL RING, BRADING.

Shop Locally.   Tel. Brading 46

Trevor Newnes, Butcher 1996

(GP) "Fanny Dowden worked for Riddick's and Jolliffe's. He would push a two wheeled handcart laden with freshly baked bread and cakes for delivery up all over The Mall, down Hornsey Rise and back along New Road. No wonder folks kept fit or became exhausted."

c. 2014

Comparative view looking north, early 20th century and 2017

Deacon's shop. Liberal Party Committee Rooms for the election campaign of Sir Godfrey Baring who was elected the Member of Parliament for the Isle of Wight 1906-10. He failed to be re-elected in 1910 and 1918.

2017

The Wheatsheaf (est. 1768) in 2009

The centre of Brading 2004

At the Bull Ring

(FTJ) "Previous to the demolishing of the cottages there was a pavement, or wide footpath, with a slight gradient, from the grocer's shop down to the shoemaker's (which was the Post Office). From the footpath there was a rough grass verge sloping down to the main road, which at that time was a lower level than it is at the present time. The width of that verge gradually diminished to nil as it reached the lower end. At almost opposite the draper's shop the footpath was so much at a higher level than the main road that one had to ascend two or three stone steps at that point to reach the footpath. That was changed at some later date by a considerable raising of the main road level. The iron bull ring itself, which weighs

about four cwt., was taken up. Otherwise it would have been buried in the course of raising the height of the road. That was the end of the old rough grass verge and there is now the buildings and footpath with its new look."

Two very early (c.1880) photographs of the Bull Ring showing all the old buildings

(FTJ) "The old Malt House, which stood derelict for many years at the lower side of the Bull Ring was used in days gone by for converting grain into malt for brewing purposes."

(BPM) 1888 "During the month of February, a soup kitchen on a small scale has by the kindness of some ladies been carried on in the Parish. Twice a week 8 gallons have been made and dispensed to the holders of tickets at a cost of 1d the quart. We hope that the soup has been acceptable."

(FTJ) "The Malt House and another row of old cottages near it were all demolished to provide a site for the New Town Hall. In one of these old cottages was a Soup Kitchen."

An early photograph, c.1880, showing the Malt House and Redstone's Bakery.

An extract from the 'Isle of Wight County Press and South of England Reporter' in February 1903: 'Erected by the Town Trustees at a cost of £1,100, Brading's new Town Hall, commemorating Queen Victoria's Diamond Jubilee, was opened by Mrs Oglander of Nunwell on February 11th. Subsequently Princess Henry of Battenberg opened a Bazaar to clear the debt remaining on the building.'

Queen Victoria's daughter, HRH Princess Beatrice, arrives at Brading's New Town Hall to open a Bazaar to raise money for the building in 1903.

Village pageant/drama in the New Town Hall 1911

Hospital Sunday Parade in the Bull Ring. Johnson's Restaurant in the background.
Between 1902 and 1918

Brading Town Band and men with collecting boxes for Hospital Sunday

Town Hall and Bull Ring. Brading. I.W. 483

Kelly's Directory in 1904: A New Town Hall has been built, the site for which was given by the vicar, the Rev Edgar Summers BD.

The New Town Hall and carved plaque on the front 2008

The iron bull ring, which still shows signs of wear caused by the bull straining at its tether ropes as it was baited by dogs. The practice of bull-baiting, once a fashionable sport, was made illegal early in 1835. According to the diaries of Sir John Oglander, the Governor of the Isle of Wight would donate 5 guineas for the purchase of the bull to be baited; the meat was afterwards donated to the poor of the town. The Mayor attended this ceremony in full regalia and a dog, known as the

2017

Mayor's Dog, would be decked with coloured ribbons and set on the bull after the proclamation had been made.

(JL) "Will Walker played the cornet in the Town Band. Mr Riddick used to conduct the Brading Orchestra. When I was a child I remember going to the concerts, the Town Hall was absolutely full and Mr Riddick would carefully hand up the soloist onto the stage and she would stand

Brading Orchestral Society 1906

and sing. I used to play in the orchestra, when I left school. I played violin. First of all I learned to play at the council school. I used to enjoy it and when I was about 14 or 15, I went into Brading Orchestra."

The Brading
Town Band
c.1870

The 5th man
(with piccolo)
left from man
with his hand
on the drum,
is William
Riddick

The Brading Town Band. (At Nunwell, about 1902)
Front row, far left — William Riddick senior (with piccolo) then William Riddick
junior (with conductor's baton), Mr S Bulley (left of drum), Sir John Oglander (with
walking cane, right of drum), then F C Corbett (with brass instrument, son-in-law of
W Riddick senior). Just below the right urn James Riddick (with trumpet, son of W
Riddick Senior), in front of James is his brother, John C Riddick (with clarinet).

Brading Home Guard during World War II 1939-45

Kelly's Directory 1904: The present (New Town Hall) entrance is a temporary one, and it is hoped that in time funds will be forthcoming to erect, in harmony with the main building, a suitable porch with ante-room or rooms to hold the town library, which has at present insufficient accommodation in the Old Town Hall.

Notice on the wall is an appeal to raise £2000 for heating and repairs to the New Town Hall. Tony Lock and Len Ballard outside c.1965

Turning into West Street

(FTJ) "Another chapel was Warder's at the other end of the street, past the Malt House where is now the Town Hall. The services here were very orderly. Mr W Warder, son, led the singing and played an instrument called the Seraphim, like a piano. His mother must have been Mary Toms, one of the first Bryanite preachers."

(MP) "The Brading 'Bible Christians' were founded by William Warder and Mary Toms in 1824. They married on 5th January, 1824, at Brading. Mary Toms came from Tintagel in Cornwall. She was born 1795 and came to the Isle of Wight as a Bible Christian preacher in 1823. Both died in Brading - Mary in 1850 and William in 1866. Their first indoor preaching Chapel was where the Public Conveniences were in West Street. The Bible Christian Chapel, now the Methodist Chapel, was built in 1867 after both William and Mary Warder had died."

(FTJ) "Brading also possessed two blacksmiths, one of these was also a shoeing smith. It was great delight to watch them at work, especially to watch a horse being shod. Mr Stay, the shoeing smith, was often called upon to mend a boy's broken iron hoop. This he did quite cheerfully and all for the charge of 1/2d. Mentioning hoops makes me think of a favourite occupation for the boys of my day. We would run miles, trundling our hoops, the boys' hoops were iron ones, the girls' were wooden ones. It would not now be a safe occupation, having regard for the motor traffic. Motorcars were unknown in those days. Marbling, too, was a favourite game, and this was often played on the highway – there was no fear of being knocked down by a fast moving car."

(KW & CB) "When we got to school there, there were horses there being shod, a blacksmith there, Stay's. I always remember old Mr Stay made us some hoops, metal hoops, what we used to call 'scurgers' we played marbles and whipping tops, there were no cars then."

The demolition of the dust cart shed on the site of the old smithy. March 1996

(JL) "My sister Jean went to the Church School in 1941 'cause the Council School was so busy. The Smithy, by the Council School, was taken over by the soldiers who used it for doing repairs."

School Garden created on the site September 1992

Known as Summers Hall, this building still exists as a private residence with an inscription on the front saying it was enlarged and restored in 1909.

Sunday School. (Rev Summers in centre)

(BPM) January 1889

"We are glad to announce that we are able to use the building in West Street, so centrally situated for both ends of our Parish, for Church purposes and we propose to call it 'The Church Hall' Our Mothers' Meeting will in future be held there and we hope to find that the increased space will bring increased attendance: the room was found at the last meeting delightfully warm and it was well lighted."

Edgar Summers, Vicar

THIS BUILDING
WAS ENLARGED AND RESTORED 1909
AS A MEMORIAL TO
THE REV EDGAR SUMMERS. B.D.
VICAR OF BRADING 1884 1906.
BY WHOM IT WAS ORIGINALLY PURCHASED
FOR USE AS A CHURCH HALL.

2017

The mural was painted on the wall of Summers Hall by Joe Fereday of New Road. The mural shows historical connections to Brading with symbols. It was 16ft high by 18ft wide, took a month and was completed in August 1958.

Willow Tree Cottage (formerly Camden) in August 2001 prior to demolition. Four 2 bedroom terraced cottages were built on the site

2017

View north east from a postcard posted 1912

(JR) "At the Senior School I went to, there was just under a hundred, Council school over a hundred, so you had 200 children on and off going to school. A lot went to Mr Bulley's apparently because folks liked his discipline so much, youngsters came from Shanklin and elsewhere. As a young boy they turned that school into a domestic science one for cooking, you could see the girls from Bembridge and St Helens come up here once a week, they used to wear white aprons up the road and they wore little white caps. They didn't care how far they went in them days at our school. All the farms came to Brading School. St Helens used to come to Brading through the marshes, up to there in mud, and sit in it all day. On the Oglander's estate they all came in and there were three families used to walk in from the bottom of Broadway, Sandown."

(JM) "Mr Lots (Head 1930-1946) was our headmaster, one summer he said, 'Well it's a nice day we'll go for our country run'. We'd go up the Downs and round the fields and we had to bring something back with us, and I'll always remember, I found an acorn that had rooted, so I brought this back, this tiny little tree. 'Course I used to have to tend it every day at school, and when the holidays came, take it home and look after, which I did, but I didn't look after it, 'cause it died. So I wasn't very popular then."

(LW) "The Heads of the village's two schools are commemorated in Rose Close and Hawkins Close, along Coach Lane. My father remembers Mr W A 'Skipper' Rose as the best of the old-fashioned type of village schoolmaster (Head 1911-1930). The school was his whole life. He would stay behind well after hours so that children could continue to play cricket or football or hockey (sticks for which he paid himself) in the playground; and though strict at times (a heavy military cane across the base of the fingers would leave them numb for some time). He rewarded good work out of his own pocket. 'Prize for you' for a good answer meant a penny at the end of the day; 'Special prize' was a sixpence, no mean sum in those days. When boys went swimming from the school, they would walk (unaccompanied) across the marshes from near the Yarbridge crossing to the beach at Yaverland; and at the end of school Mr Rose on his motor-bike would arrive to see them safely on their way home with a penny each for refreshments. Later he acquired a motor car (an

Austin 7), and would take ex-pupils, several of whom remained friends with him well after they had left his charge (among them my father, Evan Jolliffe, Percy Buckett, and Dennis Cooper, whose father ran the laundry up the Mall) on expeditions to places of interest."

(JH) "The school used to have a master there, 'Skipper' Rose. You could cheek him outside, he'd give you a clout round the ear, but you had it when you went to school on the Monday, he had you and he'd wait till you get in the classroom and sit down 'Now let me see, which boy had all the cheek?' He'd know who it was and he'd say, 'Come out and have some toffee.' Well toffee was a cane and many a time a chap from Alverstone, Alfie Attrill, would cheek him. 'Come out and have some toffee Attrill'. He went out, held his hand out and as it came down, Attrill grabbed the cane, that was enough. I've never seen a master get so mad in all my life. He got the cane, grabbed Attrill, turned him upside down over his knee, he lambasted him. We always respected that man. There was one lad there, lived up on The Mall, on Linden Terrace, same as we all did, he was forever coming to school as they blew the whistle, go in and soon he was gone. One day around playtime, the master found he was missing. He issued us out with a wooden hoop to go and look for him down by Morton Farm. The idea was if we could see him we'd throw the hoop and trip him up and half a dozen of us would have about 6 hoops on him, 3 pulling in front and 3 behind. 'Course when we got him back to school he had a damn good 'tasing'. He'd be about 10 or 11, good old days, we had some punishment then, we respected him for it."

West Street looking north c.1900

The Old Slaughter House now a private dwelling

(JS) "I remember cows being taken to the slaughterhouse in West Street. When I was at the church school I remember seeing Mr Minter, a butcher from Ryde, and chaps with sticks going down Wall Lane (Quay Lane now) to get a steer from the marshes. I'd hide and wait to see them bring it up and watch and follow them to the slaughterhouse. Everyone kept a pig."

(JH) "I went to Brading Council School, by the old blacksmith's shop in West Street. When we had pigs, Oscar Brading and Sam Jacobs ran the slaughterhouse and they used to kill 'em down there. In the mornings we used to get up early about 6 or 7 we used to drive them down there. There was no traffic about and very often when we got on the Bull Ring, a dog appeared and off they took. Father was nervous but we always rounded 'em up alright and got 'em down there. And many a time when I was a boy going to school I've seen cattle going in there and they called us boys down. They used to thread a rope through the door there and we used to pull this steer through the door as tight as we could and its head went down on a block and years ago they used to kill 'em with an axe. We never seen it done 'cause we were outside the door, but we used to help pull it through."

2017

Frederick Bench postman and Parish Sexton for 28 years delivering to Tortola Cottage. c.1900

(JH) "Down West Street, next to 'Lightning' Wright then 'Doughie', then you had the Butcher brothers George and Sunny. They lived opposite me down West Street there where Miss Sandy lived, three old thatched cottages. The first one, we used to call the three bears, was 'Musher' Coombes, 'Bosher' Miller and 'Chatty' Jones. They always called them the three bears, the kids did."

(JL) "It was rumoured that 'Musher' Coombes sold his wife. He probably had 'cause he was a real rough character."

Returning to the Bull Ring

Audrey Finlay in front of Redstone's bakery c.1910

Postcard posted 1923 showing Bonn's chemist shop, draper's and Redstone's to the left, Lloyds Bank in the front room of Shirley on the extreme right. 'Ye Olde Wheatsheaf' sign and the Conservative and Unionist Club can be seen on the left.

The Bull Ring Brading.

(BH) "Mr Bonn's, the Chemist's, had a little gate on it that was closed when he died and Mr Smith built on where the Fruit Cabin was, and that was then the Chemist."

(RW) "Around the Bull Ring: another of my father's employers was Mr S V A Burden, who sold bread (not at that time baked on the premises) and groceries from a shop at the foot of The Mall (the first shop on the left as you came down from the Mall into the Bull Ring) and sold these goods to, among others, the military personnel who occupied Bembridge Fort during the summer months. So spare a thought for a lad pedalling a heavy old bicycle with a box over the front wheel up on to Bembridge Down!"

(MP) 1880 Mary Sime had a small Dame School at Brading House.

The
"PIPE SHOP"
High Street.

TOBACCONISTS & CONFECTIONERS.

BARKER and DOBSON'S
HIGH-CLASS CONFECTIONERY.

A small SWEET RATION ?—
Make it BIG quality.

(FTJ) "The shoemaker's shop is now, and has been for many years, our local Post Office and news agency. I can remember some of the names of the people who occupied the cottages that were demolished, but not all. One I can especially remember was Mr H Huck. He was our local barber. He had a wooden leg. I also remember we used to pay him 2d for a haircut and 1d for a shave. Mrs Huck, his wife, was a remarkable woman. When she was left a widow she brought up a large family. For several years she carried on a general business in the High Street."

(JH) "Of course, we had all the old locals down the street there. We used to get quite a lot of fun out of them. Heard of old 'Mappy'? - Charlie White was his real name, he used to collect the swill for Fred Trott on The Mall. He used to keep pigs and go all around Brading and collect the swill and if we wanted a bit of fun we'd wait for him on the Bull Ring there. There wasn't a lot of traffic about. We used to undo the nuts on his cart, just check the wheel, and he would come out and get on the cart and pull away, and bang on the ground and the language! You'd never heard anything like it. He couldn't speak properly, the first thing he'd say, 'That b.......Harbour done that' or 'b.......Webb' or 'b.....Trott'. I laughed. Then there was a carrier from Sandown, Erne Taylor, and when the Bull Ring was in the middle of the road he used to pull up there every Monday, Wednesday, Friday. I think it was one

of the first old Fords that came out. He had a rope up the back one day, so we got this rope out tied it on the back of his lorry and on to the Bull Ring and waited, and, of course, you know what happened, don't you? Poor old chap, dear, dear!"

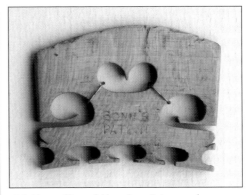

Mr Bonn (Bunn) the chemist was also an accomplished musician. He patented this four footed violin bridge.

(JS) " The first car I remember in Brading was Johnny Bonn's, the chemist."

Mains water supply arrived in Brading in 1906

Cover for the 'Brading March'

Brading Down's Reservoir 1954

Turning into New Road

(BH) "There was a pub called Robin Hood (which became the Conservative Club), my great great grandmother Bronwen's pub, that's where my mother was born."

Brading Conservative and Unionist Club 1930

(BH) "I remember the Conservative Club, what I called 'The Big Ladies of Brading' in the Conservative Club were Mrs Fairclough, Mrs Finlay, Miss Black used to come. Mrs Glass used to collect the money, there was also Mary and Frances White."

Smith the chemist moved from the building in the two photographs to the Bull Ring

(BH) "I always remember Mr Alladine, the pharmicist. Nobody went to the doctor, you'd go to Mr Alladine and say 'I don't feel very well, got a bad tummy or a headache'. He'd say, 'Would you like to sit down and I'll make you up a bottle of medicine'. He was wonderful really, used to charge you a shilling, or something like that for the medicine. It was cheaper than going to the doctor's."

Coronation Parade for George V 1911

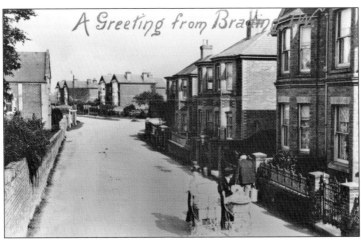

(BH) "George Wilkins was the taxi driver and he used to keep his cars up in the garage which was backing onto my wall, used to keep the horse and carts there (Dadwells?), and one Sunday morning I heard a terrific noise and jumped out of bed and rushed to the window and I saw all these sheep going down the road. I put some clothes on and dashed down stairs and shut the gates. I thought 'that's funny there is nobody with these sheep. What's happened?' So I ran down to stop them going down the High Street and I managed to get all the sheep into the Wheatsheaf, there was a closed in car park, there was a brick wall. I got all these sheep in there and George Wilkins came up the road, he said 'Morning Bett doing a bit of sheep minding?' They were Maddocks' sheep that had escaped. I asked George to mind the sheep while I phoned Maddocks. He didn't come down for three hours, he never even said thank you!"

(JH) "I always went to the Methodist Church along the New Road there. I went morning, afternoon and evening when I was a boy. I always used to go to Sunday School and chapel there. Old Sunday School teacher, Harper her name was, we used to call her 'LaLa'. She lived next to the Doll's Museum, nice old lady, if we didn't attend on a Sunday or even the afternoon, - (we may go down the railway station, see the steam engines or something) - my father knew before we got home if we hadn't been to Sunday School. She'd go up there and tell him!"

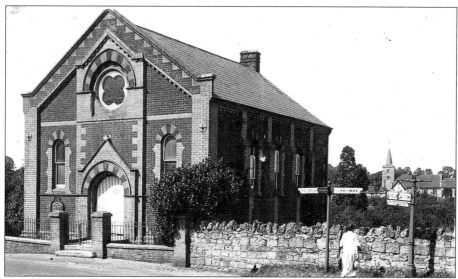

The Methodist Church c.1900 opened in 1867 as The Bible Christian Chapel.
Following the Methodist Union in 1932, it became known as The Methodist Chapel

(FTJ) "There were also two Breweries. One was known as Clare Wright's, he also ran one of the pubs. The other was at Yarbridge. Both of these have been demolished."

Brading Brewery, known as Clare Wright's, at the junction of New Road and Station Road c.1910

View towards New Road (Methodist church on far right). Postcard posted 1906.

BH) "My great aunt was Alice Bronwen, her father built the first pair of houses in Station Road. Lawrence Bronwen, my great uncle got killed, he was on a pushbike coming out of Nunwell and a car just ran into him, just dead! It was 1934, I think. I always remember that day because I practically lived in Fernlea with my great aunt and uncle was always home at 12 o'clock on a Saturday and he didn't come: Auntie was getting a bit agitated. Next thing we saw was this stretcher being carried in with him on it. They brought home the body. Terrible shock, I shall always remember that. I remember Station Road was just fields and allotments. There was a big gate and a kissing gate across the top of Station Road. When deliveries were made to the station the big gate had to be opened.

(FTJ) "There are many inhabitants of Brading who remember the green fields of Lower and Upper Furlongs - the quite extensive Furlongs' allotments which in their heyday were a beauty to behold. They will remember that from the Chapel corner down to the railway station there were just two pairs of houses. For years un-numbered, there was, standing on the right hand side of the road as one approached the station, one solitary elm tree. Station Road was a very bleak spot in those days, as folk who made there way to and from the station would find. Eventually one other building was added to the other two pairs. This was the house named Melbourne, built for Mr James Riddick, and following that another private residence. That was set between the two pairs. This was followed by the building of much needed council houses which have filled all the rest of the allotments on the one side of Station Road and the one field on the other side."

(JR) "There were only the Victorian houses in Station Road, Station Gardens was all allotments, where you go down the footpath to the Station, that was all allotments, you could go Saturday or Sunday morning and every allotment was being cultivated. There were 50/60/70 allotments over there. There was only two lights (oil lamps) down the railway, so it was a bit of a long trip down on a bad day."

AUTOMOBILE ENGINEERS,
Repairs of every description—A.A. Garage

Berry's Garage
(BRADING) LTD.

(Corner Station Road and New Road).

TAXIS for TRAINS

| Phone— Brading 225. | | Boats, Island Tours, Etc. |

Wall Lane Garage

Berry's Garage provided fuel, wedding cars, taxis and repairs up until the late 1960s

2017

(BH) "There was a blacksmith at Annerley who used to shoe all the big cart horses. In Wrax Road there is a gate and a lane that used to take them to the blacksmith's around the back."

(KW) "'Puddy' Newman did car repairs and when he was at Annerley he had a penny farthing bicycle hanging on the wall."

In 1907 Brading's first telephone exchange was established at Culver Cottage. Trunk facilities were introduced to enable calls to the mainland in 1909.

1905 New Road had no pavements

(BHi) "The New Inn c.1907 with Frederick and Florence Wood and their seven children. All four boys survived the First World War, one in the newly formed Air Force who flew as an air gunner over the trenches, two in the navy and one (unfit for military service) who worked in the accounts office of the Isle of Wight Railway."

Elm
House
today

2017

(CB) "I remember the shop on the corner of Wrax Road, old Miss Herbert, where Pat Deacon later lived, that used to be a little shop you could buy sweets. There used to be a great huge elm tree stuck outside on New Road."

View north at the bottom of Wrax Road

Early 20th century photograph

(JR) "When they built the bungalows in Wrax Road they found five wells on the land and opposite at The Mall by the Doctor's was a well, and two in the High Street."

2017

(JS) "Up in the fields beyond the back of the bungalows now in Wrax Road, there's a well and brook that runs down under the end house in the garden at the side, under the road, out into Lower Furlongs. In this brook there, all kept nice and clean, of course, was a lovely watercress bed, beautiful watercress it was, they used to sell it. There was a lady worked for them, name of her was Hinks and her son, Jim, lives in Brading now. I was out in the end house then, she used to call me and throw me over a bunch of watercress. When she was over there cutting it, she'd come down with her boots on gathering it. She was as good as any man."

View from New Road towards Wrax Road c.1950

Adverts from 1950s
Town Guide

The view from similar viewpoint today

Comparative view looking north along New Road c.1905 and 2017. Baker delivering bread. Garden walls removed and rebuilt to facilitate pavement c.1970

New Road replaced the Mall as the main route to Sandown and beyond in the 1860s. This prompted lots of new house building.

1905 Mr Redstone driving a horse and cart

Road widening and provision of a pavement c.1970

(GP) "From 1942 the army was in Verona. Two chaps there used to come over as they knew I was fishing down the river, they'd spend two or three evenings with me catching roach and dace, it was all free then, they proper enjoyed it. There were about twenty men all told in the house. They'd manned a gun down at Yarbridge in that little pill box. They had a machine gun there, always two or three men there on the look out."

Molly and John Pewsey lived at Verona from 1971 until 2014.

Craiglochie, now St. Nicholas, was built by the Black family and modelled on a Scottish hunting lodge. Miss Black was well known as a piano teacher and was church organist and choir mistress at Yaverland.

2017

Metal plaque outside St Nicholas

(GP) "I did gardening for Miss Black (at Craiglochie) I did gardening for her—she had five or six big plots down there. Her mother had a shop when I was a kid just below the butcher's shop, Miss Black's mother had a sweet shop there."

2017

Joe and Molly Fereday lived at Yarborough House New Road. Joe (1917-2001) taught at Portsmouth College of Art and Design and was an artist and engraver producing many Island views and the mural in Summers Hall. Molly taught at Sandown High School and produced enamelled work including the Mayoral chain for Brading and items for Holy Trinity Church, Bembridge.

(GP) "There were other houses along New Road, half way between Greenhills and Yarbridge, two houses there that the soldiers had, officers in one, men in the other."

Photograph c.1890 showing houses being built along New Road

Postcard of Yarbridge dated 1925

At Yarbridge

The changes to the Lincoln House building over the years. Before traffic lights were installed.

This was the only shop open in Brading on Wednesday afternoons in the 1970s when 'early closing' was observed in all other shops.

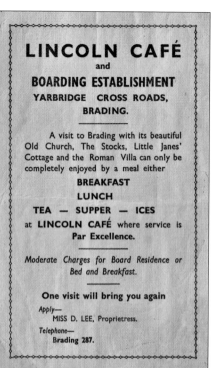

Albert and Pat Deacon's wedding day outside Lincoln Café 1950

(GP) "Esdaile Richardson (the painter) used to live in where Arnolds do in a little cottage there by The Anglers (now The Yarbridge). Used to have all his paintings in a big shop window round the corner there."

Esdaile Richardson (born 1897) was a prolific artist painting many views of the Island and abroad. He exhibited at the Royal Academy and Raphael Tuck and Sons produced series of Esdaile's paintings as postcards. Little Jane's Cottage is from 'The Garden of England' series.

(JH) "Mr Guy at Yarbridge, he had a workshop there, next to The Anglers, used to make sails, deck chairs and things like that. Twice a year my father and youngest brother Stan, we used to load up deck chairs and go to Westhill cricket ground."

The Yarbridge Inn 2017.

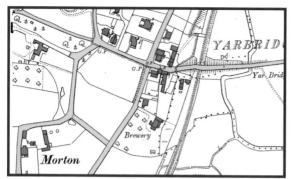

The old brewery at Yarbridge, on a site immediately south of the 'Yarbridge Inn', was first known as the Wrexham Brewery. It was later called The Yarbridge Steam Brewery and the Isle of Wight Brewery.

1908 map detail

Bottle label

Looking north. Mr Harry Pocock with horse and the old brewery building and chimney to the right.

Cask Label

Letter Heading

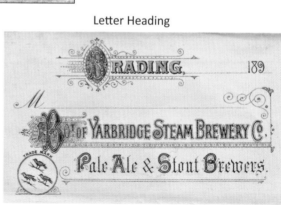

Turning into Hornsey Rise and The Mall

Munns' Family celebrations at Limekiln, then Nutbourne

(JM) "The Munns' had the lime kiln over The Mall there at Hornsey Rise, that was where father was born in Nutbourne, I'm clear on saying that he was brought up there between the lime kilns and the farm (part of the Greenwood Estate)"

2017

Brading Congregational Church c.1905

2017

The view today and an early view of the churchyard at the rear of the church c.1905. Burials were registered 1847-1974

(SEW) "My grandmother, a widow, started the Congregational Cause in her house in the High Street. My father took a great interest in the chapel that was commenced on The Mall. I often as a child walked up with him to see how they were getting on, and at the finish (1847) we met the first minister, Rev R H Smith, his wife and young children with nurse whose name I remember was Jane Cotton. They were come to live under the chapel, very nice premises facing the cemetery. Mr Mark Linington and my father were his deacons. The hymns used there were Watts Psalms and Hymn books, all in one volume. A bass viol, violins and flute were their musical instruments."

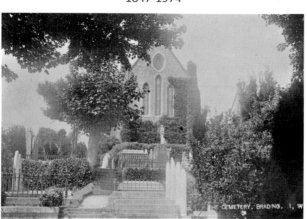

Transfer printed design applied to all the church china

View east of the Congregational Church showing the road to Newport and, to the left, the roof of the Mall Board School. From a postcard posted 1908

THE ANNUAL ENTERTAINMENT

ON BEHALF OF THE

AGED AND NEEDY OF BRADING

WILL BE GIVEN ON

THURSDAY, DECEMBER 18th, 1884,

IN THE MALL BOARD SCHOOL.

CONCERT TO COMMENCE AT 7.30.   ADMITTANCE BY TICKET.

Reserved Seats, 1s.   Front Seats, 6d.   Back Seats, 3d.

Programme.

GLEE ...	" I see them on their winding way "	
SONG	... " Great Grandmother "	*Molloy*
	MISS MUNNS.	
VIOLIN SOLO	" The keel row," air and variations	*Farmer*
	MR. J. BUNN.	
SONG	... " Forty years ago "...	
	MISS DADSWELL.	
DUET	..." Larboard Watch "	
	MESSRS. SAVAGE AND FLETCHER.	
SONG	" Some Day "*Miss & Corbett*	*Wellings*
TRIO	... " Fair Flora decks "	*Danby*
	MISS WHEELER, MESSRS. BULLEY AND SEYMOUR	
SONG	... ...	
	MRS. MUNNS.	
GLEE	..." Ye spotted snakes "	*Stevens*
SONG	... ...	
	MISS BURT.	
DUET ...	" What are the wild waves saying ?" ...	
	MISS CORBETT AND MR. BULLEY.	

SONG ...	... ...	
	MR. SAVAGE.	
SONG ...	... " One story is good until another is told " ...	*Lee*
	MR. RIDDICK.	
VIOLIN SOLO ...	... ' Home, sweet home," air and variations ...	*Dubois*
	MR. BUNN.	
SONG ...	... ...	
	MISS WHEELER.	
GLEE	" Parting and meeting " ...	*Mendelssohn*
SONG ...	... ...	
	MR. E. TURTON.	
QUARTET ...	" Profundo Basso "	*Bliss*
	MISS WHALE, MISS WHEELER, MESSRS. BULLEY AND SEYMOUR.	
SONG ...	... ...	
	MRS. MUNNS.	
DUET	... " Friendship "	
	MISS WHALE AND MISS WHEELER.	
SONG ...	... " Anchored"	*Watson*
	MR. BULLEY.	
GLEE	" In the lonely vale of streams "... ...	*Callcott*

GOD SAVE THE QUEEN.

Tickets to be had of Messrs. Redstone, Riddick, Seymour and Walker, Brading; and Mr. Turton, Sandown.

85

Procession outside the Mall Board School to the service and burial of Mr George Corbett in 1912 at the Congregational Church

(MP) "The British Day School for Dissenters, started in 1850 was enlarged in 1877. Pupils paid one or two pence a week. Pupils came from far and wide as many as 200 at one time."

Gathering of pupils past and present and a few elders to celebrate Mr S Bulley's retirement after serving for nearly fifty years in 1900.
(MP) "During that time, 3000 pupils had passed through the school."

(FTJ) "At the other end of the Mall stood the Mall Board Schools. This comprises of two buildings, one for the senior scholars and one for the infants, or primary. The senior school consisted of one very large room, one class-room, two cloak-rooms, and two toilets, one of each for boys and one of each for girls, and one entrance hall. The primary school was only one large room, and one cloakroom. These were the only schools I ever attended and that being from the age of five years until I was fourteen. Mr Samuel Bulley was the headmaster. He was a really wonderful man: a strict disciplinarian, but always kind. Always just. As a singer with a good base voice, he was often called upon to use his ability in that way at the very popular concerts organized and sustained by the Brading Orchestral Society. He was very keen on the tonic sol-fa system of music. We had regular lessons of this in school; Mr Bulley was not only headmaster of the day school but was also superintendent of the Congregational Sunday School. In connection with the day school he formed a fife and drum band. This band was utilized in heading the procession of Sunday School scholars when holding their annual treat, and outing, to some place on the Island. All these and other activities in which he was engaged was done under the following handicap – he had only one arm. How well I remember his ability in sharpening the ordinary lead pencil. The handle of an open large-sized pocket knife would be tucked under his armpit and the pencil worked on to the knife. Another method he used was a block of wood with a depression made in the centre, over which the blade of an old time "cut-throat" razor was fixed. On this he would bring the lead pencils to a fine point. To we children, watching, either of these operations were followed with great interest, with me, and I expect many others, never forgotten. The senior school came to an alarming end, which happened after its use as a school. I should explain here that the construction

Mr Samuel Bulley
1834-1918

of the building was somewhat unusual. Dwelling accommodation for a caretaker was provided, part of which formed the basement of the school, the remainder being a semi-detached adjoining the main structure. The alarming end, to which I have made mention, happened in the early hours of one morning when the whole of the south end of the school collapsed. My brother with his wife and family were in residence at the time of the occurrence. Fortunately, no one was hurt."

Mr Bulley with his class

Mrs Munns at Cookery School (In the Mall School building) 1920. They took the
cooked items around the village for sale.

A view north along The Mall 1909

Note the house down on the right: It backed onto Sydney Terrace and no longer exists. There was once a shop there, run by a Mr Stanton. The building to the right became the 'Brading Hygienic Laundry'.

2017

(FTJ) "But I think my chief delight was to stand there and, each Sunday, watch the Salvation Army march by. In those days Brading had a quite strong Corps of the Salvation Army. Their citadel was the building which is now the Hygienic Laundry. On Sunday an open-air meeting would be held at the Bull Ring, after which, headed by their very good brass band (complete with the familiar Salvation Army flag and drums), the members, and anyone who cared to follow, would march up the hill to the citadel and there hold their service. How well I remember those occasions when I awaited the approach of that procession. Sometimes I was taken into the citadel. I loved it and ever since have had a great admiration for the Salvation Army and for the work they do."

1929 Frank Jolliffe (the driver) with Peter Wetherick

Hygienic Laundry Workers. 1943.
Left to Right: Joan Taylor,
Irene Webb,
Margaret Nobbs, Ivy Nobbs

(BH) "The Hygienic Laundry kept people very busy. It was a thriving business. Jack Rock's sister took it over when Miss Wood died."

Hygienic Laundry Workers.
December, 1950.
Left to Right :
Mr Herbert, John Bowbrick,
Reg Langstaff, Algie Sears,
Jack Harbour, Mr Cooper
(Part Owner)

(JH) "The laundry had to go on a 3-day week, I think it was just after that polio scare we had in the 1950s and everybody cleared out, cause there was no work, hotel work everybody gone and they all had to sign on the dole. I had some good mates - three from the laundry got killed in the War."

Three pictures showing the laundry (and Prospect House formerly a pub 'The First and Last') before and during demolition c.1980

(JH) "I started work at 13 at Brading Laundry, mind you there was nothing about then, it was either farm or there. Being a big family - 6 of us- we was always wanting money. I used to go there weekends, perhaps I'd take a parcel to Sandown. Miss Wood then owned the laundry. She'd say "Would you take this parcel to Sandringham Hotel, serviettes and things like that, after I'd done that I use to go inside and help out especially in the summer I used to get a few shillings for it, she used to send mother down some money for what I'd done, but she always gave me 1/6 or 2/- for me pocket. Then when I got to 14 I left school. She came down, before I left school, 'Could he start at the laundry?' So I started at the laundry as a van boy. I went

through everything there. Then the time came for the army and when I came back I continued in the laundry in the boiler house and that's where I stayed for 35 years until they sold up. I remember the German girls working there Margaret, Helga. Several of them married in the village, like young Cracknell, Helga. There was Margaret, married a chap in Ryde, name of Herbert, another married Danny Wheeler, he was a local boy and there's quite a few around still. Miss Wood and Miss Flux, they were connected to the Salvation Army and that's how they started the laundry off. Next door was an

old pub (The First and Last). I was putting some footings in the old garden at the back there, I dug up a couple of pewter measures, they used to make the whiskeys with, one I stuck a fork through and that was spoilt. I found quite a few bits and pieces, then I learned it was a pub years ago."

R Cartwright Lithograph c.1830

(JR) "Mr K Day the stationmaster lived at The Manse."

(KW) "As nippers during the war, where there were stables by the rushes there, once when we were rabbiting we found a shell. We reported it to The Manse up on The Mall, 'cause the army was in there."

View of The Manse today

Early postcard of Bank Cottage (covered in ivy) and the view today

2017

(BH) "Bank Cottage was once a pub called 'The Rising Sun'."

(FTJ) "Situated at the top of a steep hill, from the Bull Ring to the Mall, there is, on the right hand side, a terrace of five houses: to reach them one has to ascend some half dozen or so stone steps. How well I remember those houses because No 1 of that terrace was the first home, that as a child I remember, and was for several years. The name then was Mall Field Terrace. It may not be now, so many old houses are re-named. The name of the occupiers of the other four cottages in the terrace I can easily recollect, even after all those years. As now, there was a boundary wall separating the front gardens from the highway. This used to be a favourite spot for me, one of my occupations being to collect a couple or three garden snails and get them to 'race' along the top of the wall which had a nice smooth surface. Sometime the 'racers' would, for a change, be woodlice."

Evelyn Cottage before (in 1986) and after demolition in 1991

(MP) When Evelyn Cottage was demolished, builders digging foundations for the new Evelyn Cottage "were digging right down, and right down they found the lime there and, in actual fact, they reckoned that it had been a Roman lime pit many years ago. Someone found a Roman coin in it when they were milling about "

(JS) "Perce Snudden was killed when a branch broke on a tree when he was collecting firewood for his mother. He lived opposite Little Jane's cottage, end one of Linden Terrace. Their daughter Blanche Homewood worked for the Browns at Beechgrove."

Little Jane's Cottage c.1900 from a glass negative. Reverend Legh Richmond was curate of Brading and Yaverland between 1797 and 1805. He later wrote moral stories including 'The Young Cottager' based on Jane Squibb who died of consumption here but her Christian faith sustained her to the end.

(JH) "Miss Runt was in Little Jane's. Before then there was a woman in there, she was blind and my father used to look after the garden. I used to go in there weeding. When war broke out – zoosh she was gone! She had the garage made into a doll's house for her child. But she just disappeared like that when war broke out, don't know if she was German or what."

(MP) "The original date of this cottage is unknown. However, a thatched farm tenant's cottage has existed on this site since the 16th century."

Jack Harbour was born on The Mall, Linden Terrace, 1922. (JH) "There were 10 children, we had 3 bedrooms, scullery, kitchen and front room, there was plenty of room there. I slept in the back bedroom with my brother when he came along and the 3 girls in the middle room and Jim, the youngest one, he came along when the girls had married, well one of the girls had."

(JH) "At the back of Linden Terrace where I lived, there was quite a long garden. Kept pigs, ducks, chickens, everything up there. Mr Gould was there before he used to live at the Red Lion in Brading. Old Mr Percival, his father had it and my father took it over when Percy Gould's dad died. It's quite a big piece of ground. There was an old house there years ago, I can't find the history of it, but the walls are still there. I can't remember it. All I can remember is the old chalk wall and the ducks used to lay their eggs on top of it."

(JH) "In Linden Terrace the only way into the loft was in through Number 9, the very end, up into the stairs and up into the loft, right up to Number 1. At night time when you laid in bed it was just like racehorses going up through and squeaking, you never heard anything like it. Of course when the rat people come they had to get permission to get up into Number 9 to get up there and bait it. I'd never go up there, it must have been alive with them."

2017

Trott's Shop

(JH) "Going back to 'Porky' Hollis, he was a big man, huge, he couldn't do his boots up where he was so fat, but every night he'd go to Ryde about 5.30 – 6 o'clock on the bus, he used to have his drink in Ryde, come back about 9 and finish up in The Wheatsheaf on port and that. Well the next day us nippers used to go into the shop and torment him. He'd sit behind there and have his dinner and that. 'Hello Mr Hollis' we'd say, 'Hello boys what can I do you for?' and Phil Wade, he was a prankster 'Have you any broken biscuits?' 'Yes, yes, how many would you like?' 'Well mend 'em then!' Well that was enough, oh dear, oh dear! He went over to Ma Wade's, we had a 'tousing' for that. Another day he went in and asked if he had any wild Woodbines, 'Yes, plenty.' 'Well tame them,' he said to him!"

Brading Rifle Club

Formed by Mr Mason of Yarbridge: Opened by Joan Oglander. The range was situated in the chalk pit at the top of Down Road. The club met on Monday evenings, May - September, until closed down in 1939: The range and club hut was then taken over by the local Home Guard and Club rifles and ammunition were impounded by the Police. The last Chairman was C Harris, Secretary, V R Redstone.

2017

(FTJ)"I remember some old cottages that stood at the top of Wrax Hill, on the site where stand the dwellings, Woodbine Cottages (or Terrace), The old cottages stood further back from the highroad than the present ones. The rear of the buildings was near to a field which was a higher level than the cottages, consequently there were no back gardens."

(BH) "I remember Mary White and Frances White, they were sisters but lived separately in two huge houses, and they never spoke to each other. One lived in Hill House the other lived in Greenhills."

2017

(JH) "I knew the old lady, a Miss Chivers. She gave me a bond and two cards when I left and joined the army, I carried it all through Italy, Africa, all over, still got the cards. Marvellous old woman and her sister married Chick Lucas. My first leave from the army I went down to Belle Vue cottage, they were both there, I think she'd moved in. Annie Smith was the housekeeper. I was sat in the sitting room there along the old fashioned fires, all of a sudden I saw this mouse coming out. He came out and sat on the table there. I picked my cap up like to kill him. Oh dear! You should have heard her 'That's my friend you mustn't touch it!' I thought, 'dear, oh dear'. Then next minute there was more coming out there. I thought there must be a regiment in there!"

(JS) "Dr Chick Lucas lived where the surgery is now (Bellevue). He wore a top hat and he had a little trap, and a dog running behind, thought it was a lurcher. He was a lovely man...a good doctor. Then he married Miss Chivers and they went up to Bellevue Cottage, done that up and lived there."

(FTJ) "At the entrance of Beechgrove is the place where used to stand one of the three public drinking water pumps. Inhabitants of Brading who were not fortunate to have a pump or well of their own, had perforce to fetch any drinking water from one or other of those pumps. At that time there was no piped supply of water in the town. I well remember, as a little chap going from my home, on the Mall, with my father, to that particular pump, he with a pair of buckets and I with my small can. A pair of buckets of fair size filled with water, which has to be carried a fair distance, especially uphill, is not the easiest of tasks. To make it easier each bucket would be suspended, one from each end of a wooden shoulder frame called a yoke, or another simple method was to use a hoop. Placing the buckets one on the left, one on the right of oneself; the hoop encircling the body, would be placed on the rims of the buckets: that, of course keeping the buckets of water clear of the legs when walking, greatly helped in transporting the load."

Early postcard c.1910 showing Beechgrove, once the home of local doctors Peter and Jane Brand. Peter served as Liberal MP for the Isle of Wight from 1997-2001

2017

(JS) "I lived in the New Road and behind me was fields. Where the Vicarage is now there was a Mr Harvey and he had a smallholding place and he kept a few chickens and turkeys and a pig and a cow. He had a lovely little trap and we used to go about in it. That was a lovely place there."

Hawthornedene, originally called Hawthorne Villa, and nowadays The Vicarage in The Mall, was built in 1857 by Mrs Rapkin's great grandfather Barnabus Barton. In 1864 Barnabus presented the house to his daughter, Francis Jane, aged 18, on her marriage to John Grimes Harvey. The Harveys had 10 children, one died as a baby, two sons died at sea and have their memorials in St Mary's churchyard. Originally the main entrance to Hawthenedene was from the Bull Ring/ New Road to what is now the rear of the Vicarage.

The Hospital Sunday Banner was made by Mrs Palmeter of Hawthornedene.

2017

(MP) "Miss Trattle's Ladies School was at Stoneham in the 1860s and in the 1870s, Mrs Mabel Duboyne had a school there."

(BH) "Dr Hay came, lived opposite in Stoneham, he came from Cowes, before the war. His wife was a Fardell, had that place out by the Roman Villa. He was a dear little man but she was a..... My Fred had a motorbike and sidecar which he parked outside. She used to come up 'Mr Barrett would you mind moving your motorbike and sidecar the Doctor can't get into the Garage'. My Fred used to say you could get a tank in there!"

(BH) "My great aunt left me this house, Rosebank. I was 12 years old when she died. We didn't live in it for quite a long time. My father did it up just before the war and I was about 15 or 16 years old when we moved here".

(BH) "I first remember this house Rosebank when I was two or three years old. My great aunt Alice Bronwen used to bring me round. The house was then empty, been empty for many years. Her father built the first pair of houses in Station Road and she used to bring me round. It was so quaint a place and out the back was all cobble stones and always primroses and pink roses in particular. There were two huge greenhouses with vines, one of them in particular used to pick 500 bunches of grapes and fruit trees at the top of the garden. It was a lovely garden which I loved. It was empty because her father had built these new houses so they closed it up and moved there. When we were children we used to call it the ghost house. There are supposed to be four ghosts in the house. I've never seen them. One is supposed to be great aunt Wee, Alice Wheeler, my great aunt's mother. The house was an undertakers in the 1840s. There used to be a stone building at the top of the garden, well, that was the workshop. The hearse used to stay in the bottom and they made the coffins in the workshop. Apparently they used to lay the bodies out in the other room, because it's a cold room."

Cover Illustrations
Top: 'Brading' Barth and King engraving 1797
Bottom: 'Part of Brading Harbour' F Jukes 1796

Cover Quote GP

MP Molly Pewsey
1930-2014

JH Jack Harbour
1922-2007 Interview 1995

JR Jack Rock
1917-2009

FTJ Fred Trueman Jolliffe
1886-1976

CB Edwin (Chick)
Buckett 1926-2010

BH Betty Howell
Interview 1996

GP George William Pocock
1910-2003 Interview 1995

HW Herbie Wetherick
1918 –2002 Interview 1996

JL Joan Legg
1921-2004 Interview 1997

KW Keith White
1926-2013 Interview 2000

Acknowledgements

The Molly Pewsey Archive

Brading Town Trust

Brading Town Council

Chris and Pam Ball Collection

Paul and Eileen Eccles

Mr Gordon Wheeler

Mr Brian Berry

Mrs Barbara Creed

Linda Allen (cement works photographs)

Mrs Barbara Hillman (New Inn picture and information)

Mr Dave Cassell (Gas showroom picture)

Mr Neil Johnson (Nancy Stay photographs)

Maps reproduced with the permission of the National Library of Scotland

Down to the Coast, East Wight Landscape Partnership

We should like to thank all those that have helped and contributed to the compilation of this book

SEW Miss Sarah Emma White 1844-1932

JS Jessie Squibb 1905-1997

AKM Audrey Kate Mursell 1916-2004

CW Clifford Webster

JSc Jim Scott

JM John Munns 1929-2012 Interview 2000

LW Lawrie Wallace

BPM Brading Parish Magazine